LIVING
PAT

Learning from the Saints

Christopher Mc Camley

All booklets are published
thanks to the generosity of the supporters
of the Catholic Truth Society

"I fully confess to the Lord God that it has been rash enough, if not even impudent in me, to have dared compose a treatise On Patience, for practising which I am all unfit, being a man of no goodness. It is fitting that those who address themselves to the demonstration and commendation of some particular thing, should themselves first be conspicuous in the practice of that thing...for fear their words blush at the deficiency of their deeds."

Tertullian

 First published 2018 by The Incorporated Catholic Truth Society 40-46 Harleyford Road London SE11 5AY Tel: 020 7640 0042 Fax: 020 7640 0040

ISBN 978 1 78469 560 6

Contents

Introduction

Fruits of the Spirit

Fruits grow from seeds, and seeds are found within fruits. We live in a world of tremendous technological advancement. We have explored the inner workings of the atom, and sent probes into the furthest reaches of the solar system and beyond. We can modify the genetic structure of a plant to improve its yield and crop resistance. Yet, we cannot produce a single seed from scratch. This is true of spiritual "seeds" as well. In our own lives it is God who plants the seed of love within us all; we cannot produce that seed ourselves. But with our choices and actions and free will we determine whether this seed will blossom into virtues, and ultimately grow into spiritual fruits. "Where a man sows, there he reaps: if he sows in the field of self-indulgence he will get a harvest of corruption out of it; if he sows in the field of the Spirit he will get from it a harvest of eternal life." (*Ga* 6:7-8)

The imagery of fruit and seeds appears often in the Bible. In the beginning, man is told to be fruitful and multiply. It is a forbidden fruit that leads to our downfall when we try to grasp something not meant for us. But it is a seed that will lead to our salvation. "And I will put enmity between you and the woman, and between your seed and her seed; he shall bruise you on the head, and you shall bruise him on the heel." (*Gn* 3:15)

When a seed is planted we have to trust it will grow – we care for it, nurture, feed, water and protect it – but we cannot keep digging it up to check it. Spiritual fruits require trust in God. The fruits of the Holy Spirit all reveal an aspect of God, at least by analogy. When we speak of God by analogy it goes both ways: sometimes we apply a human term to God, to help us to understand him; other times, we apply an aspect of the divine to ourselves. When we talk of patience, is it an attribute of God we apply to ourselves?

The one fruit

All of the fruits of the Spirit are a single fruit, St Augustine of Hippo (354-430) tells us in his commentary on St Paul's Epistle to the Galatians. Why does St Paul use the singular? Because they are all aspects of the one fruit, which is love. When we say "God is love", we are not speaking by analogy or metaphor, but something simple and true. St John in his first letter writes:

> God is love, and the one who abides in love abides in God, and God abides in him. By this, love is perfected with us, so that we may have confidence in the Day of Judgment; because as he is, so also are we in this world. (*1 Jn* 4:16-17)

We are Christians, baptised in the love of Christ, with the life of God within us, and we reveal this by our love for one another.

St Paul, in his first letter to the Corinthians, tells us what this love is like when it is made perfect in Christ:

> "Love is patient, love is kind. It does not envy, it does not boast, it is not proud. It does not dishonour others, it is not self-seeking, it is not easily angered, it keeps no record of wrongs. Love does not delight in evil but rejoices with the truth. It always protects, always trusts, always hopes, always perseveres. (*1 Co* 13:4-7)

What is the purpose of a fruit, in terms of the parent plant? The purpose is to give sustenance to others and by so doing to spread the seed further. And this is true of the fruits of the Holy Spirit. The artist Picasso expressed it well: "The meaning of life is to find your gift. The purpose of life is to give it away." Each of the saints exemplified that. St Thérèse of Lisieux (1873-1897), the French Carmelite nun, said "Jesus, help me to simplify my life by learning what You want me to be – and becoming that person."[1] What she became was "love in the heart of the Church."[2]

Our own sins

You may have decided to read this book because patience is something you struggle with. We all seem to have our own natural inclinations towards different types of sin, which should make us slower to judge others. It's easy to think some sins are worse than others, when we've never been tempted in that way. For some it is greed, or longing for power, or a particular form of lust; for others laziness, anger, impatience. Each of us has our own particular temptations to overcome, and the struggle for victory bears fruit in a particular way. The Catechism tells us "The fruits of the Spirit are perfections that the Holy Spirit forms in us as the first fruits of eternal glory."[3]

Although the fruits of the Spirit reflect different aspects of the one fruit that is love, they build upon and rely upon each other. Patience requires self-control, and kindness in dealing with others. Sometimes, when we conquer a sin, the virtue we develop will bear fruit in a different way. The person who is naturally patient may never see the spiritual fruit of patience grow in him. The fruit tree grows stronger in the face of a wind; it must put down deeper roots. We may continue struggling with patience, but bear fruit in generosity and kindness. 'All things work together for the good of those who love God' (*Rm* 8:28).

As you move through this book, we'll look at what exactly is meant by patience as a fruit of the Spirit and how patience is an aspect of the life of God himself. We will explore how important it is not to flee from or avoid the struggle, but to accept it, endure it, overcome it, and as a result grow and bear fruit. We'll examine how Christ used parables to show that patience is about accepting God's will and living according to God's time, and not ours. Through the example of holy men and women, from the time of Abraham to our own time, we will consider how the Holy Spirit shone forth in them in the fruit of patience, whether in lives of suffering and martyrdom, or in marriage and vocation. Finally we'll look at how we can use prayer and self-examination to help us develop a deeper understanding of patience, and how we too can learn to live in God's time.

Patience

What exactly do we mean by patience? The dictionary tells us it is the bearing of misfortune, pain, provocation or annoyance, without complaint, loss of temper or irritation.

It is quite possible, indeed common, to practise patience driven by what St Augustine calls "the lust of the world"[4] – the wicked man who waits patiently for the widow to default on her loan so he can seize her property; the gangster who endures much pain in plotting revenge; the abuser biding his time to seduce. These are examples of a type of worldly patience, far removed from the workings of the Holy Spirit.

The spiritual fruit of patience comes from patience practised by and for love, with faith and in hope. The bible uses two words for patience in the Greek, *makrothumia* and *hupomone*. *Makrothumia* is patience with people, while *hupomone*, is putting up with things or circumstances. *Makrothumia* is especially related to love, while *hupomone* is especially related to hope. It's also helpful to understand their opposites. The opposite of *makrothumia* is anger or revenge, whereas *hupomone* is opposed to cowardice or despondency.

The distinctions are useful, because it helps us to understand why we sometimes need to respond differently. Being patient with a person can be very different from being patient with a situation. St Augustine writes:

> Much has been said with regard to love, without which in us there cannot be true patience, because in good men it is the love of God which endures all things, as in bad men the lust of the world. But this love is in us by the Holy Spirit which was given us, and from whom comes love, and of whom comes patience.[5]

Adel Bestavros (1924-2005), a leading lawyer in Egypt and a deacon of the Coptic Orthodox Church of Alexandria, described the fruit of patience very well when he said "Patience with others is Love, Patience with self is Hope, Patience with God is Faith."[6]

St John of the Cross

The cell door cracked open. Once again John was dragged out and brought to the refectory of the monastery; he wasn't there to dine with the other friars but to be beaten and mocked. "Teresa is dead, and the reform with her," he was told. It was Spain in 1577 and St John of the Cross had been kidnapped by some of his Carmelite brothers who were opposed to the reforms introduced by St Teresa of Jesus (1515-1582), the saint from Avila who reformed the Carmelite Order. John would spend nine months locked in a tiny cell in the monastery in Toledo, deprived of food, human company, and spiritual support before escaping with a rope of sheets in the middle of the night.

John had endured much suffering in life. His father, Gonzalo, came from a wealthy family of silk merchants. However, when he married John's mother, Catalina, who was an orphan, he was rejected by his family and forced to work with his wife as a weaver. He died in 1545 when John was about three years old. Just two years later, John's older brother, Luis, died, probably as a result of the poverty in which John's family lived.

Whilst suffering would have made others bitter and resentful, in John it produced the fruit of great patience. John associated the poverty of his family with the great love his parents had for each other. With St Paul he could say:

> I have learned to manage on whatever I have, I know how to be poor and I know how to be rich too. I have been through my initiation and now I am ready for anything anywhere: full stomach or empty stomach, poverty or plenty. There is nothing

> I cannot master with the help of the One who gives me strength. (*Ph* 4:11-13)

There are two aspects to John of the Cross's captivity that reveal his patience was something more than mere human endurance: a fruit of the Holy Spirit. Firstly, it was loving and productive, and secondly he chose when to act, to effect his own escape.

It's one of the paradoxes of Christianity that we find life in death, freedom in captivity, patience in action. For St John of the Cross, the nine months were a period of intense growth, like a child growing in the womb. And his life and action serve as a guide for us. John didn't just endure and suffer, for there is no benefit in those things in themselves. John followed the advice of St Bernard of Clairvaux (1090-1153), the primary reformer of the Cistercian order, who wrote: "The quiet and silence that is enjoyed in solitude, force the soul to leave the earth in thought, and to meditate on the things of Heaven." His physical captivity in darkness became a symbol of the journey of the soul seeking the Lord, and being sought by him. Whilst held a captive the patience of St John would bear fruit in the most beautiful mystical poetry:

> One dark night,
> fired with love's urgent longings
> – ah, the sheer grace! –

I went out unseen,
my house being now all stilled.

I abandoned and forgot myself,
laying my face on my Beloved;
all things ceased; I went out from myself,
leaving my cares forgotten among the lilies.[7]

John did not endure his captivity forever. When the time came, he escaped. This too is an aspect of the patience of the Holy Spirit, for it is an active patience, a patience with urgency, a patience that searches for the time of God. Ultimately this is the key to patience as a fruit of the Spirit – it is trusting that you are living in God's time, and acting to bring it about. Endurance can come to an end when it becomes bad for you. W.B. Yeats (1865-1939), Irish poet and Nobel Prize winner, said it well when he wrote: "Too long a sacrifice can make a stone of the heart".[8] Endurance must end, if it's within our power, when it's bad for another person, when our endurance allows someone to continue committing a sin against us. St Bernard wrote "patience is not good, if, when you may be free, you allow yourself to become a slave."[9] Ending our endurance, challenging the sinner, is an act of love for the other person, and an aspect of the fruit of patience.

Growing through Struggle

Most of us, we hope, won't be imprisoned by our fellow Christians. But we will all find ourselves in situations that severely test our patience. So, what should we do? Should we try to avoid the occasions that lead us into impatience? Sometimes we can see the cause of our faults and try to fix them. If we get impatient because we are late, perhaps we plan on leaving earlier. If that photocopier that always jams annoys us, maybe take responsibility for getting it serviced. If we've soap in our eyes and there's no towel because someone did the laundry, maybe it's a sign we should be doing more around the house.

Those are situations where we are the cause of our own impatience, but often we have less control. Many saints and spiritual writers testify to the importance of not avoiding the struggle in spiritual and moral growth, not fleeing the field of battle.

Thomas à Kempis

Thomas à Kempis (1380-1471), the German religious who authored "The Imitation of Christ", one of the most popular Christian books on devotion ever written, reminds us that there are many things in life that try our patience and that we need to accept them. We have to try to practice the virtue of patience, to help us gain the fruit of peace. He writes:

> Patience is necessary in this life because so much of life is fraught with adversity. No matter how hard we try, our lives will never be without strife and grief. Thus, we should not strive for a peace that is without temptation, or for a life that never feels adversity. Peace is not found by escaping temptations, but by being tried by them. We will have discovered peace when we have been tried and come through the trial of temptation.[10]

St Thérèse of Lisieux

How can we endure the great suffering that may come our way if we cannot cope with the small annoyances of life? The great Carmelite saint, and Doctor of the Church, Thérèse of Lisieux (1873-1897), shows us that the way to great sanctity is the little way, the overcoming of little faults, motivated by love. She wrote of one of her own annoyances:

> For a long time my place at meditation was near a Sister who fidgeted incessantly, either with her rosary or with something else... I cannot tell you to what an extent I was tried by the irritating noise... I remained quiet, but the effort cost me so much that sometimes I was bathed in perspiration, and my meditation consisted merely in the prayer of suffering.[11]

We all have things that try our patience: people who stop at the top of an escalator or wait until all their shopping has been scanned before looking for their wallet or purse; people who put forks where the knives should go; or who mispronounce "scone". These things are the pebbles in our spiritual shoes, and they can incapacitate us in ways that more significant problems don't.

If we make a mental list of what tries our patience, we have to remind ourselves that they are "people who…". When we face up to our impatience we start with people, and the acceptance that we are placing ourselves above them. The person at the top of the escalator may have vertigo, they may be lost, unsure where to go. My two seconds of anger may be the two seconds they need to cope with things. Why do we think that our time is more important than anyone else's?

How did St Thérèse deal with her impatience? What drove St Thérèse on, was not stoicism, nor a stubborn desire to conquer her faults, but love, love for the sister in Carmel. And this is what turns the practice of a mere virtue into a fruit of the spirit and shows the presence of the Holy Spirit in our lives. With St Thérèse this would flower in the patience revealed during her long suffering and difficult death, but even more, in her patient endurance of the dark night.

St Thérèse suffered from tuberculosis. She spent over a year in pain and gradual physical decline. She was also assailed by severe temptations to doubt her faith. Her dark night derived from doubt of the existence of eternity. To these doubts she did not give assent with her mind or will but instead kept going by a deepening of her faith. She said to her sisters, "If you only knew what darkness I am plunged into."[12] It was the long practice of patience in small things, that allowed the Spirit to carry her through the darkness. St Thérèse described a sense of separation from God in terms of a total lack of consolation. She fought the temptation to despair and made frequent acts of faith in Jesus Christ and God's love for her. She wrote: "while I do not have the joy of faith, I am trying to carry out its works at least. I believe that I have made more acts of faith in this past year than all through my whole life."[13]

While the dark night is usually temporary, it can last for a long time. The "dark night" of St Paul of the Cross we are told lasted almost fifty years. And in recent times, we have come to know that the dark night of St Teresa of Calcutta, whose own name in religion was chosen in honour of St Thérèse, may have endured from 1948 almost until her death in 1997, with only brief interludes of relief. These are saints who were sustained by the fruit of patience.

Father Willie Doyle

Father Willie Doyle, SJ, MC (1873-1917), was an Irish Jesuit priest who was killed in action during the First World War at the Battle of Passchendaele, a word that still resonates with mud and death, and terrible suffering. Fr Willie was a brave man who never ran from a battle, whether in war or in the spiritual life. He had tested his valour though many years of spiritual struggle and mortification. As a young novice he had written in his diary that he was sure he would die a martyr's death, and he would prepare for this by a life of "slow martyrdom by earnest hard work and constant self-denial". The love which drove Fr Willie to his death, going to the aid of other soldiers who had been wounded, was a love developed in countless acts of self-sacrifice. He struggled himself with impatience, but, as in all things, he never sought the easy way. He wrote:

> Are you not foolish in wishing to be free from these attacks of impatience, etc.? I know how violent they can be, since they sweep down on me at all hours without any provocation. You forget the many victories they furnish you with.[14]

God plants the seed and the struggle helps it take root and grow; the grace of God brings it to fruition. God supports our struggles with great patience, for he is the patient One. When we embrace the fruit of patience, we are embracing something right at the heart of God.

The God of Patience

When Moses led the Israelites out of captivity in Egypt, they spent forty years wandering in the desert. We think of those forty years as a time of great endurance – and indeed it was – for God. He endured their complaints, their ingratitude, their infidelity, their sheer inability to understand what he was offering them, the loving relationship he desired for them. He was patient with them, and he wanted them to learn patience – to learn to live according to his time, to his plans. It took forty years for them to be ready to enter the Promised Land. And in the book of Joshua God reminds the Israelites that what he has done for them is pure gift: "I gave you a land where you never toiled, you live in towns you never built; you eat now from vineyards and olive-groves you never planted." (*Jos* 24:13)

It is a good way to understand the relationship between the virtues we practice, and the fruits of the

Holy Spirit. We can struggle to practice patience, and struggle we must, but our struggles will only bear fruit when we finally place ourselves within the plans and time of God. Irish author C.S. Lewis (1898-1963), creator of the fantasy series, the Chronicles of Narnia, tried to describe the relationship between faith and works, and between works and grace, as being like the two blades of a pair of scissors – can we say which blade does the cutting? Is it a pointless question? In some ways, but perhaps the more important question is "whose hand holds the scissors?"

St Paul in his Second Letter to the Corinthians reminds us clearly whose hand guides the scissors:

> We are only the earthenware jars that hold this treasure, to make it clear that such an overwhelming power comes from God and not from us. We are in difficulties on all sides, but never cornered; we see no answer to our problems, but never despair; we have been persecuted, but never deserted; knocked down, but never killed; always, wherever we may be, we carry with us in our body the death of Jesus, so that the life of Jesus, too, may always be seen in our body. (*2 Co* 4:7-11)

Living in God's time

Patience is about timing – patience, as a fruit of the Spirit, is ours when we live in accordance with God's timing, not ours – or rather, when we make his timing our timing.

St Dominic Savio (1842-1875), the young student of St John Bosco, was noted for his holiness as a child. He died from pleurisy when he was only fourteen. He was the first person of his age group canonised without being a martyr, on the basis of having lived a life of heroic sanctity, and the youngest until the canonisations of Francisco and Jacinta Marto, the visionaries of Fatima, in 2017. When asked what he'd do if he was told he had only an hour to live he said, "I'd carry on playing football". This is living in God's time.

St John Fisher (1469-1535) was the great bishop and cardinal executed by order of Henry VIII during the English Reformation for refusing to accept the King as Supreme Head of the Church of England, and for upholding the Catholic Church's doctrine of papal primacy. When told he was to be executed in the morning, he apparently turned over in bed and went back to sleep. That is living in God's time.

There's a story told of Pope St John XXIII by Monsignor Loris Capovilla, his private secretary. Every night, just before going to bed, Pope John would kneel down and put his trust in God and say, "I've done the best I could in your service this day, Oh Lord. I'm going to bed. It's your church. Take care of it!" That is living in God's time.

Most of us are familiar with the quote from St Augustine: "Lord, make me chaste – but not yet". It's often quoted as if Augustine were recommending the sentiment, promoting hypocrisy and promiscuity. In reality he was describing the attitude many of us have to morality and holiness. He wrote:

> But I, in my great worthlessness, had begged You for chastity, saying "Grant me chastity and continence, but not yet". For I was afraid that You would hear my prayer too soon, and too soon would heal me from the disease of lust which I wanted satisfied rather than extinguished.[15]

We can all understand that attitude. Whether it's dieting or exercise or praying we often aspire to a goal while being unwilling to take the steps to attain it. In essence we say to God "I accept your plan, I know your timetable, but I'm not yet ready for it." The fruit of patience comes when we begin to live according to God's timetable for us.

The phrase "restless patience" is a good way to understand this fruit of the spirit. It describes the dual sense of being patient, of waiting, of enduring, and yet being paradoxically impatient for God to do something, and for ourselves to act. When Augustine said "You have made us for yourself, O Lord, and our hearts are restless until they find their rest in you"[16] he was describing his whole life, a life not marked by obvious human patience, but by a relentless search for the truth, which came to him in time. This is living with the fruits of the Spirit.

If we contrast the words of St Dismas, the Good Thief, to Jesus, with the words of the other thief, we have some sense of what living in God's time can mean. The first thief demanded, "save yourself and us as well" – do it now, follow my timetable, my demands. The Good Thief said, "Jesus, remember me when you come into your kingdom" – remember me in your time. And the Lord responded "Indeed, I promise you, today you will be with me in paradise". The Good Thief, in that moment had the fruit of patience; he was living in God's time.

We are all familiar with those verses from the Book of Ecclesiastes:

> There is a time for everything, and a season for every activity under the heavens: a time to be born and a time to die, a time to plant and a time to uproot, a time to kill and a time to heal, a time to tear down and a time to build, a time to weep and a time to laugh, a time to mourn and a time to dance, a time to scatter stones and a time to gather them, a time to embrace and a time to refrain from embracing, a time to search and a time to give up,

> a time to keep and a time to throw away, a time to tear and a time to mend, a time to be silent and a time to speak, a time to love and a time to hate, a time for war and a time for peace. (*Qo* 3:1-8)

This describes beautifully what living in God's time is like, what living with the fruit of patience can be. It is knowing that we must endure the bad and celebrate the good, and trust in God. Ecclesiastes continues, perhaps less familiarly:

> I have seen the burden God has laid on the human race. He has made everything beautiful in its time. He has also set eternity in the human heart; yet no one can fathom what God has done from beginning to end. I know that there is nothing better for people than to be happy and to do good while they live. That each of them may eat and drink, and find satisfaction in all their toil—this is the gift of God. I know that everything God does will endure forever; nothing can be added to it and nothing taken from it. (*Qo* 3:11-14)

This truly is patience, the fruit of the Spirit – eternity in the human heart, the knowledge and acceptance that everything from God will endure.

Patience of God

"Never mind, I'll do it myself" – a phrase we often use with children (and spouses or co-workers), when we are too impatient to wait for them. It is explained by our sense of our own superiority, which may be justified in regard to the particular task in hand. But really it comes from a reluctance to allow someone the time, and perhaps guidance and knowledge to develop. The paradox of God is that although he has the power and the knowledge to do all things, he waits for us. Whether in divinely designed evolution, or in salvation history, God, the eternal One, allows us to grow, to fall, to be saved in time. He emptied himself, taking on the form of a servant. He allowed us to be saved by one who was like us, in all things but sin.

Pope Benedict XVI at the inauguration of his papacy preached:

> It is not power, but love that redeems us! This is God's sign: he himself is love. How often we wish that God would show himself stronger, that he would strike decisively, defeating evil and creating a better world. All ideologies of power justify themselves in exactly this way, they justify the destruction of whatever would stand in the way of progress and the liberation of humanity. We suffer

> on account of God's patience. And yet, we need his patience. God, who became a lamb, tells us that the world is saved by the Crucified One, not by those who crucified him. The world is redeemed by the patience of God. It is destroyed by the impatience of man.[17]

The Catholic faith has an instinct for holding two contrasting things together: tradition and scripture, God and Man, justice and mercy, grace and free will, virtue and fruits of the Spirit. The paradox of patience is that we should be impatient for God, our hearts should be restless for him. Blaise Pascal (1623-1662), French mathematician, physicist, inventor, writer and theologian wrote:

> What else does this craving, and this helplessness, proclaim but that there was once in man a true happiness, of which all that now remains is the empty print and trace? This he tries in vain to fill with everything around him, seeking in things that are not there the help he cannot find in those that are, though none can help, since this infinite abyss can be filled only with an infinite and immutable object; in other words by God himself.[18]

We see the patience of God in the small events of salvation history. Consider the events of the early chapters of Genesis. God has created the universe, created time, light and life. He has created us and almost immediately we've turned our backs on him, failed to trust in him, disobeyed him. And what does he do? The creator of the universe becomes a tailor and makes clothes for Adam and Eve (*Gn* 3:21). When Cain becomes the first murderer in history, killing his brother Abel because of envy, God protects him with a special mark (*Gn* 4:15).

Jesus through his own suffering and death, and acceptance of the Father's will, is the epitome, the icon, of patience. In his parables Jesus shows us how we can – and *must* – embrace the patience of God, and enter into his time.

Parables of Patience

Jesus reveals the patience of God to us through a number of parables, and how we can and should grow in patience.

The unforgiving servant

In the parable of the unforgiving servant (*Mt* 18:21-35) Jesus responds to Peter asking how many times we should forgive someone; as often as seven times? Jesus speaks of a king who forgives a servant who owes him ten thousand talents – something like a billion pounds today. The king forgives him and wipes out the debt. The servant then meets another servant who owes him a few hundred pounds. Instead of being inspired by the mercy of the king, he demands the money immediately – the patience of God contrasted with the impatience of man. God has wiped out all our sins, has sent his son to us, and yet we cannot bring ourselves to forgive others the smallest thing.

The prodigal son

In the story, a father has two sons. The younger son asks for his inheritance and after spending all the money on wasteful extravagance becomes totally impoverished. He returns home intending to ask his father to be made one of his hired servants. The father welcomes him back, indeed rushes out to meet him and celebrates his return. The older son refuses to participate. The father reminds the older son that one day he will inherit everything, but they should still celebrate the return of the younger son because he was lost and is now found.

It's a familiar story, which we hear at Mass on the 4th Sunday of Lent each year, and a remarkable parable of patience.

The younger son is so impatient that he cannot wait for his father to die to collect his inheritance. He cannot wait to spend it, he cannot wait for a wife instead paying for prostitutes, and when famine comes he cannot wait to be paid – he wants to eat the food of the pigs. It is only when he becomes aware of his suffering that the son begins to understand what patience is. The story reveals that patience isn't to be passive – to wallow with the pigs – but to be active and redemptive, which in this case means a return to repentance, forgiveness and love.

And then we see the patience of the older son, a sort of patience – waiting for the father to die, waiting for respect and signs of love, waiting to enjoy life. The older son, no more than the young, is not living the life that God intended for him. He has turned in on himself, and found little there to please him.

In contrast, the father has found the fruit of patience. He puts up with both his children, and waits patiently for them to, as the gospel says, "come to their senses" (*Lk* 15:17). He waits in hope and is ready to act at the first sign of repentance and reaching out. And when he acts it is a great over-the-top display of love and mercy, his grace greater than any sin.

The wheat and the darnel

In this parable (*Mt* 13:24-30) an enemy plants weeds (darnel) among the wheat that a man has planted. When they both begin to grow, the man's servants suggest trying to root out the weeds, but the man points out this will be difficult and they'll end up pulling out wheat as well as weeds – best leave them until the harvest. Then they can be divided, weeds in the fire and wheat in the barn.

This parable reveals the patience of God, who lets the rain fall on the wicked no less than the good. The darnel in the story is a type of rye grass that can be hard to tell apart from wheat when they start to grow. The Lord is saying every person must be given a chance to show whether they are wheat or weed. We live in a world in which evil lives side by side with good. We can feel swamped by it. We want to complain to God about it: "Where does this evil come from?" And we are impatient to have it removed. The Lord assures us of two things: the evil does not come from him, but from the enemy; and it will be dealt with, at the end of the world.

St Augustine pointed out that the "wheat" and "darnel" also runs through the Church. He writes:

> O you Christians, whose lives are good, you sigh and groan as being few among many, few among very many. The winter will pass away, the summer will come; lo! The harvest will soon be here. The angels will come who can make the separation, and who cannot make mistakes...I tell you of a truth, my Beloved, even in these high seats there is both wheat, and weed, and among the laity there is wheat, and weed. Let the good tolerate the bad; let the bad change themselves, and imitate the good. Let us all, if it may be so, attain to God; let us all through his mercy escape the evil of this world. Let us seek after good days, for we are now in evil days; but in the evil days let us not blaspheme, that so we may be able to arrive at the good days.[19]

The talents

Consider the parable of the talents (*Mt* 25:14-30). This is a story of zealous, restless patience versus empty patience. The men with five talents and two talents set to work and have twice as much to give the Master on his return; the man with one talent hides it and waits in fear for the Master. The Lord does not want us to simply suffer and endure and put up with things. To do that is to merely return to the Lord what has been given to us. This is the difference between mere endurance and patience as a fruit of the spirit. We often have no choice but to suffer, whether its sickness, grief or deprivation, but we can choose what we do with the suffering. Do we bury it, or do we invest it?

St Paul in the Letter to the Romans wrote: "For everything that was written in the past was written to teach us, so that through the endurance taught in the Scriptures and the encouragement they provide we might have hope." (*Rm* 15:4). This is true of the parables of Jesus, but also of the lives of patience shown by the saints of old, who serve as exemplars for us. As the liturgy says, they teach us "to hope for salvation."

The Patient People of Old

Let's look at some saintly men and women from the Bible who stand out as people in whom the spirit of patience flourished, prophets of hope for salvation.

Abraham

God promised to Abraham that he would be the father of many nations. But when the promise was first given (*Gn* 12:1-3) Abraham and his wife Sarah did not have any children and were already old. Indeed Sarah laughed at the idea. God continued to repeat his promise to Abraham through the years.

Finally when Abraham was one hundred and Sarah was ninety years old God gave them their son, Isaac. Though it took years of patiently waiting, they received the promise of God. Hebrews 6:15 says of Abraham, "And so, after he had patiently endured, he obtained the promise." And yet God then asked Abraham to sacrifice Isaac to him, to test his patience. Abraham's trust in God was so great that he agreed, before the Lord stopped him.

Joseph

Joseph's brothers sold him as a slave (*Gn* 37:27,28). Though he did not understand all that was happening, he trusted God to work out his plan in his time. Joseph worked patiently and faithfully in each situation he was in. He waited for God to fulfil his promise that Joseph would be a leader of his people (*Gn* 37:5-11). He had to be patient as he believed God, even though he found himself sitting in a prison cell.

God did lift Joseph up to great power and responsibility. Not only was he a leader of his people, but he ruled over the people of Egypt, too. Patience was needed to allow God to accomplish his purposes in the life of Joseph and his family.

Job

Probably the best known story of patience in the Bible is the life of Job. To prove Job's fidelity to the Lord, God allowed Satan to take and destroy everything Job owned (*Jb* 1). Job had been a wealthy man. He lost his crops, property, cattle and servants. And then, most devastating of all, Job lost his children. However, Job did not blame God. He accepted that God had a plan and would be patient for God to reveal his plan.

Job's friends came to comfort and counsel him. They tried to find out what great sin Job had committed to deserve the punishment he received. Job would not admit to any sin. Job knew that sometimes bad things happen to good people. Often people will talk about the patience of Job. He knew God had a plan and was willing to accept what God allowed in his life. In the end God restored to Job twice as much as he had in the beginning (*Jb* 42:10).

St Martha

St Martha is a saint of impatience who learned patience. Most of us have a sneaking sympathy for Martha. When Jesus came to visit Martha and her sister, Mary, it was Mary who sat at the feet of Our Lord while Martha did all the work. And when Martha asked the Lord to get Mary to help her, he famously said: "It is Mary who has chosen the better part; it is not to be taken from her" (*Lk* 10:42). Generations of writers and preachers have since then praised the contemplative over the active life. But who was it who took the initiative and welcomed Jesus into her house? It was Martha. Who was it who provided him with hospitality? It was Martha. Had Martha not taken the initiative, then the Lord may never have entered the house. Martha's problem was twofold: she allowed herself to be distracted, and she then tried to tell the

Lord to make her sister help. She had the wonderful opportunity of living in the Lord's time: she was welcoming, she was serving, but she lacked that grace to rest with the Lord, to accept his time.

If we consider the other story involving St Martha, the raising of her brother Lazarus from the dead, we see a more developed "active patience" at work. St John sets out the story in chapter 11 of his gospel. Timing is important in the telling. Lazarus is sick so the sisters send word to Jesus. Instead of coming to heal him immediately, the Lord lingers for several days, finally arriving four days after the funeral. Once more it is Martha who acts: "When Martha heard that Jesus had come she went to meet him. Mary remained sitting in the house." (*Jn* 11:20) This time it is Martha who has chosen the better part. This time she is not distracted, this time she places herself in the hands of the Lord. She had waited patiently for the Lord to come and heal her brother, and even now, after his death, her patience continues. She doesn't scold but simply asserts the truth: "If you had been here, my brother would not have died, but I know that, whatever you ask of God, he will grant you". It is similar to the approach Our Lady took at the wedding feast in Cana. She said to Jesus, "They have no wine." When Jesus tried to fob his mother off – "Woman, what does this have to do with me? My hour has not yet come" – Our Lady said to the servants, "Do whatever he tells you." (*Jn* 2:1-12)

Martha has accepted the Lord's time, and the fruit of her patience is the powerful declaration: "I believe that you are the Christ, the Son of God, the one who was to come into this world." (*Jn* 11:27). Like all of us, Martha may not understand the plans of God, why her brother could not have been saved from his illness. So she does what we must do – she talks to the Lord, she seeks understanding, she places her trust in him. In essence, she prays. So our patience must be an active patience, a zealous patience and a praying patience.

In learning to live according to God's plans and timing, there is perhaps no clearer way than in accepting suffering and martyrdom. Endurance is a central aspect of patience, and no saints reveal the fruit of patience as clearly as the martyrs.

Suffering and Martyrdom

Pope St John Paul in his Apostolic Letter, Salvifici Doloris ("Redemptive Suffering"), wrote: "Suffering is present in the world in order to release love, in order to give birth to works of love towards neighbour, in order to transform the whole of human civilization into a 'civilization of love.'"[20]

Let's look at some of the saints who have built up this civilization of love through their martyrdom, transforming suffering into the fruit of patience. Flannery O'Connor (1925-64), an American Catholic writer, feared she could never be a saint in the ordinary way, but thought maybe "she could be a martyr if they killed her quick."[21] The reality of course is that martyrdom for many comes slowly, often over many years.

Blessed Aloysius Stepinac

Blessed Aloysius Stepinac is one such martyr. Born in 1889 into a Croatian peasant family, Aloysius was the eighth of twelve children, his mother always hoping that he would be a priest. She had to be patient. At eighteen he was called up to serve in the Austro-Hungarian army in the First World War on the Italian front and taken prisoner. After demobilisation in 1919 he went off to study agriculture at the University of Zagreb. Finally, six years later he went to Rome to study for the priesthood and was ordained in 1930. Returning to Zagreb as Archbishop's secretary, he worked especially in the poor neighbourhoods, and established the archdiocesan charity for the poor – Caritas. It wasn't long before he was made coadjutor and then Archbishop in 1937. It was to be a cross for him, which he accepted in love: "I love my Croatian people and for their benefit I am ready to give everything, as well as I am ready to give everything for the Catholic Church." He took as his motto: "In te Domine speravi" (In you, Lord, I place my trust). It was to be the most appropriate of mottos.

With the advent of Nazism Archbishop Stepinac became a champion of human rights irrespective of religion, race or nationality. He helped hide victims, usually Jews, in Church properties throughout the Second World War.

1945 saw the oppression of Nazism replaced by Communism in Yugoslavia. Stepinac fought for the rights of the Church and the interests of Croatians in the larger state. He published a letter attacking the murder of priests by communist militants and was arrested for the first time. Yugoslavia's new leader, Tito, then tried to persuade him to have the Catholic Church in Croatia break from Rome, the game-plan of tyrants from Henry VIII to modern day China. The Bishops of Yugoslavia issued a pastoral letter in September 1945 calling for respect for freedom of conscience, religion, and private ownership of property, freedom for the Catholic press, Catholic schools, religious instruction, Catholic associations, and "full freedom for the human person and his inviolable rights, full respect for Christian marriage and the restitution of all confiscated properties and institutions".[22] The Communist state-run media attacked the Church, and the archbishop in particular.

Archbishop Stepinac was put on trial in September 1946 for defending the unity of the Catholic Church in Croatia, and its unity with Rome. Pope Pius XII objected to what was clearly a show trial. Prominent Jewish leaders in America said "this great man has been accused of being a collaborator of the Nazis. In reality Aloysius Stepinac was one of the few men in Europe who raised his voice against the Nazi tyranny, precisely at the time when it was most dangerous to do so."[23] In October 1946, he was found guilty after a short trial and sentenced to sixteen years of hard labour.

His experience, his suffering and his patience was shared by many bishops in Communist Europe, men like Cardinal Mindszenty, the Hungarian primate and archbishop of Esztergom, Cardinal Slipyj, head of the Ukrainian Greek Catholic Church and Cardinal Beran, archbishop of Prague. They were all vilified by enemies of the Church, and each responded with patience, truth and love.

In December 1951, Archbishop Stepinac was moved from prison to house arrest because of ill health. The authorities were desperate to get him out of the country but he refused to go. Under house arrest he continued in ministry, received visitors, and, like St Paul, wrote letters, more than 5,000. The letters are remarkable for the patience in suffering they reveal, with no anger or resentment for those who were persecuting him.

Pope Pius XII made him a cardinal in 1953, calling him, "an example of apostolic zeal and Christian strength…and especially to honour and comfort our sons and daughters who resolutely confess their Catholic faith despite these difficult times." The Yugoslav authorities reacted by breaking diplomatic relations with the Holy See and determining to silence Cardinal Stepinac. He died of ill health in 1960, but during his beatification process his body was examined and arsenic was found in his bones. Many believe he was murdered by the Government. He was declared a martyr in 1998 and beatified by Pope St John Paul later that year. Blessed Aloysius is a martyr of patience. Unlike the many martyrs of old, they did not "kill him quick". They tried to destroy his name, his reputation and the Church he represented. He remained patient with God, with himself and with others, displaying great faith, hope and love. Grant us, Lord, the same faith and perseverance in suffering for the Church.

The darkest periods of history, those bleak periods of intense human suffering, can often be lit up, however briefly, by the spark of sanctity, the fruit of patience revealed in hope and faith and love of an individual soul. A Maximillian Kolbe who steps forwards and offers his life for another, showing that in a time and place where life is thought so cheap, it is in reality of infinite value. There were few times as dark as the Nazi era, and few times where the fruits of the Holy Spirit blossomed so clearly.

While of course many Christians were murdered by the Nazis, the main focus of their hatred was the Jewish people: six million of them were murdered, in what we call the Holocaust. Their suffering was the culmination of centuries – indeed millennia – of persecution. It seems almost trite to say they are a people who have shown tremendous endurance and patience. The Spirit of God, who first hovered over the water of creation, who called Abraham into covenant, who spoke to

Moses in the burning bush, has not deserted the people he chose, and he has shown this in the fruit of patience.

The Holy Spirit in the life of non-Christians

Speaking after the World Day of Prayer for Peace in Assisi in 1986, which brought together 160 religious leaders from thirty-two Christian religious organisations and eleven non-Christian world religions, Pope St John Paul stressed the universal presence of the Holy Spirit, stating that "every authentic prayer is called forth by the Holy Spirit, who is mysteriously present in the heart of every person," Christian or otherwise.

The Pontifical Council for Interreligious Dialogue expanded on this point when it said:

> All men and women who are saved share, though differently, in the same mystery of salvation in Jesus Christ through his Spirit. Christians know this through their faith, while others remain unaware that Jesus Christ is the source of their salvation. The mystery of salvation reaches out to them, in a way known to God, through the invisible action of the Spirit of Christ...The fruits of the Spirit of God in the personal life of individuals, whether Christian or otherwise, are easily discernible.[24]

The fruit of patience was easily discernible in the life of Etty Hillesum.

Etty Hillesum

Etty Hillesum was a young Dutch woman of Jewish origin working in Amsterdam during World War II. She kept a series of diaries recording her insights and spiritual development. As war progressed she began to see life in a new way and from being a somewhat self-absorbed intellectual, she started serving Jewish refugees in a Nazi transit camp. Finally Etty, her parents, and a brother and sister were transported to Poland, and she was murdered in Auschwitz, on 30th November, 1943, at the age of 29.

Her diaries had been saved by friends and were published in Dutch in 1981, and two years later in English.[25] In them she reveals a young woman for whom the appalling conditions were not just something to be endured, but were the crucible in which her love and faith and hope grew. Blessed Titus Brandsma, the Dutch Carmelite friar who died at Dachau concentration camp spoke for many when he wrote, "Do not yield to hatred. We are here in a dark tunnel, but we have to go on. At the end, an eternal light is shining for us."[26]

Etty saw that eternal light even in the darkest places. She wrote:

> I don't feel in anybody's clutches, I feel safe in God's arms; and whether I'm sitting at this beloved old

desk now or in a concentration camp under armed guards, I shall always feel safe in God's arms.[27]

Her writings are full faith and patience:

God, take me by your hand, I shall follow you dutifully, and not resist too much. I shall evade none of the tempests life has in store for me, I shall try to face it as best I can...I shall try to spread some of my warmth, of my genuine love for others, wherever I go…I don't want to be anything special, I only want to try to be true to that in me which seeks to fulfil its promise.[28]

Patience, the fruit of the Holy Spirit, flourished in Etty. We described it earlier as patience which is productive, loving and leads to action. Etty wrote:

You have made me so rich, oh God, please let me share Your beauty with open hands. My life has become an uninterrupted dialogue with You, oh God, one great dialogue. At night, when I lie in my bed and rest in You, oh God, tears of gratitude run down my face, and that is my prayer.[29]

While many of us may feel inclined to blame God when things go wrong, like the friends of Job, Etty accepted that in a world of suffering and evil caused by the free will of men, God may not intervene to save us. Towards the end she wrote:

> Alas, there doesn't seem to be much You Yourself can do about our circumstances, about our lives. Neither do I hold you responsible. You cannot help us but we must help You and defend Your dwelling place inside us to the last...Ultimately, we have just one moral duty: to reclaim large areas of peace in ourselves, more and more peace, and to reflect it towards others. And the more peace there is in us, the more peace there will be in our troubled world.[30]

The last record we have is a postcard she threw from the train to Auschwitz. On it she had written, "We have left the camp singing." We can hear the echo of St Paul writing to the Thessalonians: "Rejoice always, pray continually, give thanks in all circumstances; for this is God's will for you in Christ Jesus." (*1 Th* 5:16-18)

Patience in Marriage and Vocation

While all of us will experience suffering in our lives, few of us will suffer martyrdom. We will have to develop holiness in the more mundane crucible of a life lived in an ordinary way, among ordinary people. Just as the demands of living with other religious in community can provide opportunities for spiritual growth as St Thérèse has told us, so marriage is often the setting for patience to grow. St Francis de Sales (1567-1622), bishop of Geneva and a noted spiritual director, writes, "The state of marriage is one that requires more virtue and constancy than any other. It is a perpetual exercise in mortification."[31] In marriage spouses compete to place each other's needs before their own – or they should. And the arrival of children can mean increased opportunities for growth in all of the fruits of the spirit, not least patience. A number of saints were renowned for patience because they endured difficulties in marriage.

St Rita

We call St Rita of Cascia (1381-1457) "saint of the impossible" because of the power of her prayers. She has a greater claim to be known as St Rita the Patient for she had much to endure. She personified the virtue of patience, and her life bore great fruit under the inspiration of the Holy Spirit.

Margherita Lotti (St Rita) was born in 1381 in Roccaporena in Umbria, Italy. She was married at age twelve to a nobleman named Paolo Mancini, the wedding having been arranged by her parents despite her repeated requests to be allowed to enter a religious community. Rita had her first child within the year. She spent eighteen years married to her abusive, violent and unfaithful husband. However, her patience, humility and love finally converted him near the end of his life. Her husband, Paolo was murdered by some of his many enemies, as part of a family feud.

Rita publicly pardoned her husband's murderers at his funeral, but his brother, Bernardo, was said to have continued the feud and wanted to get Rita's sons to seek revenge. Rita was afraid that her sons would lose their souls and tried to persuade them not to retaliate, but it was no good – they wouldn't listen. Legend tells us that she prayed to God to take her sons before they could commit the mortal sin of murder. Both her sons died of dysentery within the year.

After their deaths, Rita applied to enter the monastery of Saint Mary Magdalene in Cascia but was turned away. Rita's good character and piety were well known, but the nuns were afraid of being associated with the scandal of her husband's violent death. Once more the patience which had marked her life as a wife and mother was required. She persisted in her cause and the monastery gave her a way to get in – she had to reconcile her family with her husband's murderers first. She set about the task of establishing peace between the hostile factions of Cascia in the midst of bubonic plague, which ravaged Italy at the time.

She was able to resolve the conflicts between the families and, at the age of thirty-six, Rita was finally allowed to enter the religious community she had longed for since she was a child.

She remained at the monastery, living by the Augustinian Rule, until her death from tuberculosis on 22nd May, 1457.

St Monica

St Monica, the mother of St Augustine, was famed for her patience, with her son, with her husband and with her mother-in-law. She was married early in life to Patricius, a Roman pagan, who held an official position in Tagaste. He is said to have a violent temper and a mother who had the same.

Monica had three children who survived infancy: sons Augustine and Navigius, and her daughter, Perpetua. A source of great pain for Monica was that Patricius would not allow them to be baptised.

Like many women before her and since, Monica suffered in silence. She wrote: "Guard your tongue when your husband is angry."[32] For years Monica prayed for her husband and mother-in-law, until finally, one year before Patricius' death, she successfully converted them.

The life that Augustine began to lead caused her still greater distress. He was lazy and wayward. When Patricius died, she sent Augustine, now seventeen, to school in Carthage. He returned home to her a Manichaean, a gnostic religion that saw the world and material things as evil. St Monica acted by throwing him out of the house. At some point St Monica went to talk to a bishop about Augustine, who had now fathered a child and was living with a woman. The bishop famously told her, "the child of those tears shall never perish."[33]

St Monica followed Augustine to Rome, and then Milan where she met the bishop, St Ambrose. He it was who helped her convert Augustine to Christianity. Monica and Augustine spent six happy months together at Rus Cassiciacum, after which Augustine was baptised in the church of St John the Baptist at Milan.

They decided to return together to Africa. Monica died on the journey, at Ostia. As she neared death she said to Augustine, "Son, nothing in this world now affords me delight. I do not know what there is now left for me to do or why I am still here, all my hopes in this world being now fulfilled."[35]

Monica's persistence and her perseverance in not giving up praying for Augustine brought one of the greatest minds in human history into the Church. Her restless patience bore fruit in his conversion, and every page Augustine wrote, every sermon he preached, were written on the prayers of St Monica.

Servant of God Léonie Martin

The fruit of patience is common among the saints for whom finding the right vocation in life can be delayed and difficult. While everyone is familiar with St Thérèse of Lisieux, and the story of her impatience to enter Carmel, including directly petitioning the Pope when she was only fourteen, her sister Léonie is less well known. Léonie Martin was born on 3rd June, 1863, ten years before St Thérèse. In comparison with her sisters, who had each successively and successfully enter Carmel, Léonie led a more challenging life. She suffered illness from childhood and was somewhat isolated within her family. She'd been expelled by her school and been abused by a maidservant. Three times she tried religious life before she finally succeeded in 1899, and aged thirty-five, entered definitively the Monastery of the Visitation at Caen, taking the name "Sister Françoise-Thérèse". She died in 1941 at the age of seventy-eight.

It cannot have been easy, at the human level, coming from a family in which her parents were saints, all her sisters were Carmelites nuns and she didn't seem to fit in. And yet Léonie became a sister everyone remembered as happy, peaceful and kind, with no trace of the unhappy child, or troubled adolescent.

Léonie had the fruit of patience. She was patient with herself, which is hope. Each time she had a setback, she tried again, searching for the right place and time for herself, driven by that restless patience of the Spirit. The French writer, Georges Bernanos, author of *The Diary of a Country Priest*, wrote:

> How easy it is to hate oneself! True grace is to forget. Yet if pride could die in us, the supreme grace would be to love oneself in all simplicity – as one would love any one of those who themselves have suffered and loved in Christ.

Léonie accepted that she was different from her sisters and would not be part of the community of Carmel. But she found Christ where she was, in her pain and rejectedness, and made him the centre of her being.

She became the first and best follower of St Thérèse's "little way of confidence and love." When Léonie was accepted at the Visitation and became Sister Françoise-Thérèse, she wrote:

> I am very happy – as happy as it is possible to be on this earth. When I look back on my past, as far back as my earliest childhood, and compare that time with this, I am overwhelmed with gratitude to the Heart of Jesus, who has enveloped me in so much love, and who has placed me in this loveliest anteroom of heaven, where I shall live and die.[36]

Léonie's process of beatification opened in 2015. Her body, which lay in a tomb in the crypt of the monastery of the Visitation in Caen since she died in 1941, has now been transferred to a new tomb in the chapel where she professed her vows in 1900. Many people come to pray at her tomb including parents of children with special needs and people who struggle to find their vocations. She seems to speak in a special way to the troubled and to those who struggle to find a place in the world. St Thérèse wrote her final letter to Léonie when she was living with her aunt and uncle having made her third unsuccessful attempt to enter the convent. She wrote:

> The only happiness on earth is to apply oneself in always finding delightful the lot Jesus is giving us.

> Your lot is so beautiful, dear little sister; if you want to be a saint, this will be easy for you, since, at the bottom of your heart, the world is nothing to you.[37]

St Teresa Benedicta of the Cross

A saint who combined the struggles to find her vocation, with the endurance that led to martyrdom was St Teresa Benedicta of the Cross. She was born Edith Stein in Breslau, Germany, on 12th October, 1891, the feast of Yom Kippur. She was the youngest of eleven children in a well-respected Jewish family. She abandoned Judaism when she was about thirteen, declaring herself an atheist. Edith, like St Augustine before her, was a patient searcher for the truth. She entered the University of Gottingen, where she became a pupil and assistant of the famous philosopher, Edmund Husserl, and an exponent of the philosophy of phenomenology. This claimed to have overcome the traditional distinction in philosophy between appearance and the object itself. It was about the study of consciousness and how consciousness comes to know the essential structures of things.

Edith received a doctorate in 1916 and was one of Europe's brightest philosophers. However, both her Jewish background and her female sex, made it difficult for to progress in her career because of the discrimination rampant at the time. She was referred to as Husserl's "secretary," when in fact she was a philosopher in her own right. Edith had edited the manuscript of Husserl's book, On the *Phenomenology of the Consciousness of Internal Time*, yet Martin Heidegger took the work and credited himself with editing it.

During this time Edith describes going to Frankfurt Cathedral. She saw a woman with a shopping basket going in to kneel for a brief prayer. "This was something totally new to me. In the synagogues and Protestant churches I had visited people simply went to the services. Here, however, I saw someone coming straight from the busy marketplace into this empty church, as if she was going to have an intimate conversation. It was something I never forgot."[38]

At the end of her doctoral dissertation she wrote: "There have been people who believed that a sudden change had occurred within them and that this was a result of God's grace."[39] This was to happen to Edith. One night, while staying in a friend's house, she read St Teresa of Avila's autobiography – the whole book in a single sitting. St Teresa of Avila would not have regarded herself as a philosopher nor a phenomenologist, but she was a gifted natural describer of the human experience of prayer and God – her own experience. Edith is said to have closed the book and immediately proclaimed – "this is the truth". Edith was baptized on 1st January, 1922. She gave up her university post and became a teacher in the Dominican school at Speyer, and in 1932 became a lecturer at the Educational Institute of Munich, before resigning under pressure from the Nazis, who were then in control of Germany.

In 1934, Edith followed St Teresa of Avila and became a Carmelite nun, taking the name Teresa Benedicta of the Cross. She and her sister Rosa, also a nun, were smuggled out of Germany into the Netherlands in 1938 to escape the mounting Nazi oppression. But they were seized by the Nazis in 1942 as part of the order by Hitler to liquidate all non-Aryan Catholics after protests by the Dutch bishops against the treatment of the Jews. She and Rosa were taken to Auschwitz, and, on 9th August, 1942, she died in the gas chamber there.

Edith Stein's whole life was a search for God, for truth, which she found in the cross of Christ. At every point in her journey she was forced to make difficult choices, including the painful moment of telling her mother that she was becoming a Catholic. At every point other people intervened to delay her choices and her desires, whether it was becoming a professor or entering the Carmelite monastery. At no point did she waver. She was the model of patience and this bore fruit in her martyrdom, targeted as a Catholic Jew, yet "dying for our people".[40]

All of the holy men and women of patience we've looked at learned to live in God's time and not their own. They did this by allowing the Holy Spirit to dwell with them. And they were able to do this because they were people of prayer. The same Spirit which moved them to accept suffering and death, moved their hearts to friendship with God, developed in prayer. As we too try to discover patience in ourselves, we must ask the Lord for his help.

Praying for Patience

To grow in patience is to pray with patience. Why is prayer so important? Because without prayer we have no way of discovering when we should endure and when we should act. Without prayer we can become passive people who endure instead of restless people of patience, living in God's own time. Without prayer, St John of the Cross would have stayed in his cell of captivity until he died or rejected the reform of Carmel. Without prayer Blessed Aloysius would have abandoned his beloved Croatia. Without prayer St Joseph would have "quietly divorced" his betrothed and dare we say it, without prayer, the Virgin Mary may have muttered a quiet "no" to the angel Gabriel.

The Rosary of Patience

Among the most helpful ways to grow in patience is to meditate on patience with the Rosary. The praying of the Rosary can help lead us into God's time. As we try to rush ahead, God tells us to slow down and literally say ten Hail Marys while we ponder things in our hearts. It's rather like when we tell a person having a panic attack to take a deep breath and count to ten.

Each set of mysteries have their own link with the patience of God and his saints, but the Joyful mysteries in particular are mysteries of patience which can help us to learn how to live in God's time. St Teresa of Jesus, the great doctor of prayer from Avila, often prayed the six decade rosary which she learned from the Brigittines. So let us start with an extra mystery in the Joyful Mysteries.

The Immaculate Conception: In this mystery we consider the patience of God himself, waiting from the time of Man's first fall, through the long years of salvation history, the calling of Abraham, the election of Israel, until his patient gaze fell upon Mary, the second Eve, chosen before her conception, gifted above all others with the Spirit's gifts.

Annunciation: In this mystery we consider the patience of Mary and Joseph. Mary is called upon to become the mother of God. The timing was hardly optimal: not yet fully married, a young girl, still a virgin. Mary didn't rush in we are told, but asked the angel "how can this be?" It wasn't a rejection of God's plan, but a humble plea for understanding. It was a prayer, because this is the only way we can know what God wants for us. Is this the time to act, or the time to wait? Joseph too is a man of great patience. He did not have the benefit of an annunciation, but had to trust in Mary and a dream. He too serves as a guide for us in learning to live in God's time, to trust the people we know are close to God. He also reminds us that knowing the truth doesn't always make things easier to bear.

Visitation: In this mystery we see that patience, the Spirit's gift, isn't a passive waiting. Mary has nine months until the birth of her son, and she uses it well. She goes off to her elderly cousin, Elizabeth, in an act of mission, bringing the grace of Christ with her. Catholic tradition tells us that when the child in Elizabeth's womb, John the Baptist, leapt for joy on encountering Jesus, he was cleansed of original sin. Mary responds with her wonderful Magnificat, a hymn of praise proclaiming God's saving power in time. It is no accident that the Magnificat came to grace the Divine Office of the Church, marking each day the evening prayer of the liturgy of the hours, God's time. Elizabeth and Zechariah, too, are models of patience. They are a common type found in salvation history, the elderly couple waiting for God to fulfil his promise of a child, the barren couple made fruitful: they stand in the shadow of Abraham and Sarah, Isaac and Rebecca, Jacob and Rachel, the parents of Samson, the parents of Samuel. They represent patience and trust in God's timing, even when hope seems futile.

Nativity: In this mystery we see the simple patience of Mary and Joseph. They have been told that something wonderful is to happen – Mary is to bear the Son of God – and yet they find themselves in a stable, a cave, a place of darkness, as so often happens to followers of the Lord. In that darkness we can only proceed with trust. Mary's soul magnifies the Lord, and Joseph we call the Mirror of Patience. Consider the patience of Israel awaiting the Messiah, present at the nativity as shepherds. The place where the shepherds heard the news is known as the Tower of the Flock, and it is possible they were guarding the lambs and sheep destined for sacrifice in the temple. Instead, that night they found themselves guarding the Lamb of God. And consider the angels of God. Tradition tells us that Lucifer and the other fallen angels fell from grace because they could not accept the creation of man, the incarnation of Christ, and his birth from a woman who would be Queen of Heaven and Queen of Angels. The other angels not only accepted it, but longed for it and when it came, it was singular moment of joy which could not be contained. We often talk of the patience of a saint – consider the patience of an angel.

Presentation: Let's ponder first the patience of Mary. Mary was a daughter of Israel and followed the Law. After giving birth a woman had to be purified. After the birth of a son, for forty days "she must not touch anything sacred or go to the sanctuary until the days of her purification are over" (*Lv* 12:2-4). Mary had carried the Son of God; she had given birth to him, held him and fed him from her breast. She touched his most sacred body every hour of every day. Yet she followed the Law patiently, just as Christ, the sinless one, would later allow himself to be baptised by John. Simeon and Anna, who come to prophesy about the Christ, are the epitome of patience. Each of them lives in God's house and in God's time, waiting for the fulfilment of his promise. For them the Christ child is the fruit of patience. And so Simeon can proclaim, "Now, Master, you can let your servant go in peace, just as you promised; because my eyes have seen the salvation which you have prepared for all the nations to see, a light to enlighten the pagans and the glory of your people Israel." (*Lk* 2:29-32). Just as Mary's Magnificat is used to mark evening in the liturgy, so Simeon's Nunc Dimittus is used at Night Prayer. Each day we go to bed having seen the salvation God has prepared for us.

Finding in the Temple: In this mystery, we consider first the patience of Jesus and what it meant for him to live in God's time. For him at that time the place he should be was clear – in the temple, his Father's house. He has to be patient with his parents who are slower to understand this. And yet Jesus places himself under obedience to them, spending eighteen years at home, working as a carpenter. Why did Jesus, who is God, have to do this? He did it to show us what it is to wait, to prepare, to be ready to act in God' time. Patience is a prelude to mission.

Daily Examen

St Ignatius Loyola (1491-1556) proposes "A Method of Making the General Examen" in his "Spiritual Exercises". He suggests five sequential actions:

- To give thanks to God our Lord for the benefits received.
- To ask for the grace to know our sins and cast them out.
- To ask account of our soul from the hour that we rose up to the present Examen, hour by hour, or period by period; first as to thoughts, and then as to words.
- To ask pardon of God our Lord for our faults.
- To make a firm purpose of amendment with his grace.

The examination of our day is not a psychological investigation of ourselves; it is prayer. It is considering our day together with God, attentive to where we experienced God's call in the midst of everyday activity. Did we live in God's time or our time? Did we trust him or just ourselves?

St Teresa Benedicta of the Cross has some advice:

> Let go of your plans. The first hour of your morning belongs to God. Tackle the day's work that he charges you with, and he will give you the power to accomplish it. When night comes, and retrospect shows that everything was patchwork and much that one had planned left undone, when so many things rouse shame and regret, then take all as is, lay it in God's hands, and offer it up to him. In this way we will be able to rest in him, actually to rest and to begin the new day like a new life.[41]

Rather than simply present ourselves with a series of questions as is common in the traditional examination of conscience, we might re-read some of the texts we've read from the saints and consider how we lived up to them this day.

"Patience with others is Love, patience with self is Hope, patience with God is Faith".

Did we remember that patience is rooted in loving our neighbour? Did we retain the hope in our ability and desire to become a saint? Did we place all our faith and trust in God, the patient One?

St Teresa's Bookmark

Be thou by naught perturbed,
Of naught afraid,
For all things pass save God,
Who does not change.
Be patient, and at last
Thou shalt of all fulfilment find.
Hold God and
Naught shall fail thee,
For he alone is all.

St Teresa of Avila's shortest work, and a summary of her spiritual teaching, is a programme for life and for every day. Did we allow ourselves to be disturbed and afraid today? Or did we remember that today's problems are just for today? That meeting we're worried about today will be gone tomorrow. Etty Hillesum said "We have to fight them daily, like fleas, those many small worries about the morrow, for they sap our energies."[42] Every problem and annoyance and worry we have will pass, and only God will remain. So instead of holding on to worries and grudges and anger and frustration hold on to God, for he alone is everything, everything.

Litany of Patience

This litany by Christina Dehan Jaloway is inspired by the well-known Litany of Humility by Cardinal Merry

Del Val, Secretary of State under Pope St Pius X. It is an excellent way to meditate on how we've tried to live with patience during the day.

From the desire to control my life,

R: Deliver me, O Jesus.

From rash judgment and haste...

From impulsive decision making...

From the desire to act when I need to be still...

From the desire to speak when I need to stay silent...

From the delusion that my own ideas and plans are what would be best...

From impatience with the sins and idiosyncrasies of others...

From impatience with my own sins and slow growth in virtue...

From impatience with Your plan for my life...

From the desire to live on my own timeline...

From the fear of running out of time...

From the fear of aging and death...

From the temptation to act out of sorrow, discouragement, anxiety, or fear...

Lord, teach me to trust your love so entirely:

That I may wait upon your Word before making important decisions.

That I may not get ahead of or behind your Spirit.
That I may maintain an eternal perspective in all that I do.
That I may accept and surrender to your will for me daily.
That I may truly believe that ALL things work for the good of those who love you.
That I may radiate to others Your peace and joy which surpass all understanding.[43]

Lord God, give us the gift of patience.
Deepen our faith, strengthen our hope,
enkindle our love;
and so that we may obtain the gifts you promise,
make us love what you command.
Through our Lord Jesus Christ, your Son,
who lives and reigns with you
in the unity of the Holy Spirit, one God,
for ever and ever.
Amen.

A final thought from St Francis de Sales:

Have patience with all things, but chiefly have patience with yourself. Do not lose courage in considering your own imperfections but instantly set about remedying them – every day begin the task anew.

Endnotes

[1] Thérèse of Liseux, *Story of a Soul: the Autobiography of St. Thérèse of Lisieux,* translated by John Clarke, OCD (ICS Publications, third edition, 1996)

[2] ibid.

[3] *Catechism of the Catholic Church*, Section 1832.

[4] St Augustine of Hippo, *On Patience* (http://www.newadvent.org/fathers/1315.htm)

[5] ibid.

[6] http://www.bestavros.net/adel/Meditations.html

[7] St John of the Cross, *The Dark Night of the Soul* (Toledo, 1579)

[8] Yeats, William Butler, "Easter 1916"

[9] Bernard of Clairvaux, *De Consideratione* (Clairvaux, 1152)

[10] Kempis, Thomas, *Imitation of Christ*, (Netherlands, 1427)

[11] Thérèse of Liseux, *Story of a Soul: the Autobiography of St. Thérèse of Lisieux,* translated by John Clarke, OCD (ICS Publications, third edition, 1996)

[12] ibid.

[13] ibid.

[14] O'Rahilly, Alfred, *Father William Doyle S.J.* (Tradibooks, 2011)

[15] Augustine of Hippo, *Confessions* (Hippo, 400)

[16] ibid.

[17] Benedict XVI, Homily given at St Peter's Square, Rome, 24th April, 2005, (https://w2.vatican.va/content/benedict-xvi/en/homilies/2005/documents/hf_ben-xvi_hom_20050424_inizio-pontificato.html)

[18] Pascal, Blaise, *Pensees* (Paris, 1670)

[19] Augustine of Hippo, "Sermon 23 on the New Testament" (http://www.newadvent.org/fathers/160323.htm)

[20] John Paul II, *Salvifici Doloris* (Vatican:1984)

[21] O'Connor, Flannery, *A Good Man is Hard to Find and Other Stories* (Harcourt, Brace and Company, 1955)

[22] O'Brien, Anthony, *The Man and His Case* (Dublin, Standard, 1947)

[23] ibid.

[24] Pontifical Council for Interreligious Dialogue, "Dialogue and Proclamation" (Rome, 19th May, 1991)

[25] Hillesum, Etty, *An Interrupted Life*, (Jonathan Cape Ltd, 1983)

[26] Hanley, Boniface, *Through a Dark Tunnel: Story of Titus Brandsma* (Hyperion Books, 1988)
[27] Hillesum, Etty, *An Interupted Life and Letters from Westerbork*, translated by Arnold Pomerans (Henry Holt & Company Inc, 1996)
[28] ibid.
[29] ibid.
[30] ibid.
[31] Sales, Francis, *Letters to Persons in the World* (Aeterna Press, 2015)
[32] Esper, Joseph, *More Saintly Solutions to Life's Common Problems* (Sophia Institute Press, 2003)
[33] Augustine of Hippo, *Confessions* (Hippo, 400)
[34] ibid.
[35] Bernanos, Georges, *Diary of a Country Priest* (DaCapoPress, 2001)
[36] http://leoniemartin.org
[37] ibid.
[38] Sullivan, John (ed.), *Holiness Befits Your House* (ICS Publications, 1999)
[39] ibid.
[40] Oben, Freda Mary, *The Life and Thought of St. Edith Stein* (Saint Pauls/Alba House, 2001)
[41] Gelber, L. and Linssen, Michael (eds), *Collected Works of Edith Stein, Sister Theresa Benedicta: The Hidden Life v. 4*, translated by Waltraut Stein (ICS Publications, 1992)
[42] Hillesum, Etty, *An Interupted Life and Letters from Westerbork*, translated by Arnold Pomerans (Henry Holt & Company Inc, 1996)
[43] Jaloway, Christina Dehan, "Litany of Patience" (used with author's permission)